Charlie and the Aztecs

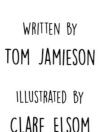

WRITTEN BY

TOM JAMIESON

ILLUSTRATED BY

CLARE ELSOM

The Aztecs are a group of people who
lived in Mexico hundreds of years ago.

OXFORD
UNIVERSITY PRESS

T0369621

OXFORD
UNIVERSITY PRESS

Great Clarendon Street, Oxford, OX2 6DP, United Kingdom

Oxford University Press is a department of the University of Oxford. It furthers the University's objective of excellence in research, scholarship, and education by publishing worldwide. Oxford is a registered trade mark of Oxford University Press in the UK and in certain other countries

British Library Cataloguing in Publication Data
Data available

ISBN: 978-0-19-276972-5

10 9 8 7 6 5 4

Paper used in the production of this book is a natural, recyclable product made from wood grown in sustainable forests. The manufacturing process conforms to the environmental regulations of the country of origin.

Printed in China

Acknowledgements
Series Advisor: Nikki Gamble

The manufacturer's authorised representative in the EU for product safety is Oxford University Press España S.A. of El Parque Empresarial San Fernando de Henares, Avenida de Castilla, 2 – 28830 Madrid (www.oup.es/en or product.safety@oup.com). OUP España S.A. also acts as importer into Spain of products made by the manufacturer.

Helping your child to read

Before they start

- Talk about the back cover blurb. What would it be like to travel back in time? Would it be fun, or scary?

- Look at the front cover. What does your child think Charlie is wearing? What kind of story do they think this will be?

During reading

- Let your child read at their own pace – don't worry if it's slow. They could read silently, or read to you out loud.

- Help them to work out words they don't know by saying each sound out loud and then blending them to say the word, e.g. *g-oa-l-ie, goalie.*

- If your child still struggles with a word, just tell them the word and move on.

- Give them lots of praise for good reading!

After reading

- Look at pages 36 to 39 for some fun activities.

Chapter One

"Mum, I've finished my homework! Can I go out to play?" asked Charlie.

"All right, Charlotte. Just don't bring any more mud inside!"

Charlie always felt odd when Mum called her Charlotte.

Potatoes
Onions
Milk
Rice
Tomatoes

Usually, everyone just called her Charlie.
Charlie **loved** sports.
She **loved** cricket.

She played football for the school team.
"I wish you were on *our* team!" said a
goalie from another school.

Charlie didn't
know it yet, but
she was going to
need all her sports
skills very soon.

Chapter Two

Charlie's class was studying the Aztecs.
They were visiting a museum to learn how
the Aztec people lived hundreds of years
ago. The museum was filled with lots of
interesting objects.

Charlie's favourite object was a beautiful Aztec headdress with blue and red feathers from rainforest birds.

"Come along, class," said Mr Jones. "There's lots more to see!"

Charlie stayed behind for a closer look.

Charlie knew she shouldn't touch the headdress but she couldn't help herself. Carefully, she picked it up and put it on her head.

Suddenly, there was a flash of light.

Charlie felt her head. The headdress had gone! She looked around. The whole *museum* had gone! Birds with blue and red feathers flew overhead in the sky.

There were thick green bushes and tall trees all around Charlie. "Where am I?" she asked, in wonder.

She was in a forest. And not
just any forest. Peering through
the bushes, Charlie could see
a village. An Aztec village!
"But the Aztecs lived
hundreds of years ago ..."
said Charlie. "That must
mean ... I've travelled
back in time!"

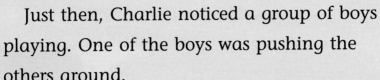

Just then, Charlie noticed a group of boys playing. One of the boys was pushing the others around.

"Are you new here?" said a friendly voice behind her. Charlie turned. It was a girl about her age.

"Yes!" she said. "My name's Charlie."

"I'm Izel," replied the girl. "Shhh. I'm meant to be doing my chores ... but I couldn't stay inside any longer!"

"I know just how you feel," said Charlie, grinning.

"Why is that boy being mean to the others?" Charlie asked.

"That's Totil," said Izel. "He's the son of Zolin, our leader. Zolin is wise and kind – but sadly, Totil is not."

"You've arrived on an important day,"
Izel went on. "Once a year, we hold a
sports contest to find out which of the
boys is the fittest."

"Don't the girls take part? That's silly!"
said Charlie.

"I'd better get going," said Izel. "Mum needs me to collect some firewood – want to help?"

Charlie followed Izel into the forest. Izel was quick and Charlie struggled to keep up.

"Hey, you're really fast!" Charlie said.

"*You* should enter that contest."

"I'm not allowed to enter," said Izel, picking up sticks and bits of wood. "Anyway, it's not a real contest. The other boys always let Totil win. He says Zolin will be cross if he loses."

"If Zolin is such a wise leader, he wouldn't want anyone winning if they didn't deserve to," said Charlie.

"Yes, but Totil is his son," said Izel. "Come on, I'll race you back!"

Izel beat Charlie back to the village.

"You're too quick for me," said Charlie, panting.

They came to a line of boys who were
waiting for the contest to begin.

Charlie thought for just a moment –
and then joined the line!

·◨◫◨· Chapter Three ·◨◫◨·

"What are you doing, Charlie?" hissed Izel.
"You know girls aren't allowed in the contest!"
　"No one has to know I'm a girl," said
Charlie, grinning. She grabbed a helmet to
hide her hair.

Izel told Charlie about the contest. It was an Aztec game called Ulama. You scored points by throwing a hard rubber ball through a stone ring.

It was just the sort of game that Charlie loved.

The crowd cheered as their leader Zolin
entered the arena. He was wearing the
same headdress that Charlie had tried on
in the museum.

Charlie stared at the headdress. She knew
she couldn't stay with the Aztecs forever. The
headdress had brought her here, so maybe
it could take her home.

Zolin gave the signal for the contest
to begin.

Charlie watched the other boys falling
over, trying to let Totil win. They looked
so silly.

Totil scored two goals.

Finally, it was Charlie's turn. She ran fast and dodged past the boys! She took her shot.

GOAL!

The crowd cheered. Now she was just one point behind Totil.

Charlie scored one.

Totil scored as well.

Charlie scored again.

"There's never been a game this close!"
yelled the crowd. Just then Charlie heard
the sound of a horn. **Game over!**
It was a draw.

"The winner will be decided by a tiebreak," said Zolin. "You both get one shot."

Totil went first.

He missed!

If Charlie scored, she would win.

"Please Charlie, miss!" said Izel under her breath.

◇·◇·◇ **Chapter Four** ◇·◇·◇

"Maybe I should let Totil win," thought Charlie as she lined up her shot.

No, she couldn't do that.

Her ball flew straight through the ring. Charlie had won! The crowd cheered.

Zolin stepped forward, looking stern. Suddenly Charlie felt very scared.

"We've never seen a boy beat my son before," he said.

"Well," said Charlie bravely, "my name is Charlie, and I'm a girl!" She took off her helmet.

"Girls aren't allowed to play!" screeched Totil. "It's against the rules. I win!"

"Not so fast," said Zolin, calmly. "Charlie won fair and square. She is the winner."

He really was a wise leader.

Totil sulked, while Izel hugged Charlie.

"Next year, I'm going to enter!" Izel said.

The crowd cheered.

"I will grant you one favour, Charlie," said Zolin.

"Can I ... try on your headdress?" asked Charlie.

Zolin looked puzzled, but smiled. He carefully handed Charlie the headdress.

"Thank you," she said. She put it on and crossed her fingers …

Once again there was a **flash** of light!

Suddenly, Charlie was back in the museum. The headdress was back on its stand.

"**Hurry up, Charlie!**" called Mr Jones.

"I'm back! Everything's back, just the way it was …" said Charlie, looking around happily.

"Or maybe not!" she said, spotting a painting on the wall. It showed Izel – and she was playing Ulama!

After reading activities

Quick quiz

See how fast you can answer these questions!
Look back at the story if you can't remember.

1) What was Charlie's favourite hobby?

2) Why did Charlie's class go to the museum?

3) What happened when Charlie put the headdress on?

4) What clue helped Charlie work out where she was?

5) What was the name of the girl Charlie met?

6) Why did Charlie have to pretend to be a boy?

7) How did Zolin feel when Charlie beat his son in the contest?

8) How did Charlie get back to the museum?

36

Talk about it!

- Do you think Izel will enter the contest next year? What do you think might happen if she did? Are there any clues in the story about this?

- How did Charlie's sports skills help her when she went back to Aztec times?

- If you were Charlie, would you want to go back to the Aztec village again?

Try this!

Imagine you found a magic hat that could take you back in time. What would the hat look like? Where would it take you?

Draw a picture of your magic time-travelling hat!

Retell the story!

Use the pictures to help you retell the story.